For Bruno, Camille, Pia, Baudouin, Maximilien, Gaspard, and Aliénor.
In memory of their grandfather Bertrand.
S.M.-H.

Original French edition:
Bernadette, petite fille de Lourdes
© 2008 by Fleurus Mame, Paris
© 2010 by Ignatius Press, San Francisco • Magnificat USA LLC, New York

ISBN Ignatius Press 978-1-58617-510-8
ISBN Magnificat 978-1-936260-09-6

Printed by Tien Wah Press, Malaysia
Printed on September, 2020 - 2nd edition
Job Number MGN 20035-03
Printed in Malaysia in compliance with the Consumer Protection Safety Act, 2008.

"Look at her, her face is covered in mud! It's disgusting!"

"She's obviously gone mad!"

But Bernadette did not care what people thought. A few days later, she began doing the same things again. When she was asked why, she answered calmly, "It's for sinners." But no one understood what she meant. The next Sunday, after Mass, the local policeman hauled her off to the judge like a common thief. Poor Bernadette!

As she stood before the judge, Bernadette's heart was pounding. What would he do to her? Would he treat her like a liar or lunatic? Worse still, he looked very strict. But the thought of the Beautiful Lady very quickly gave her courage again. After all, she was telling the truth … but the judge was not at all of that opinion!

"So it's you," he said, "the little Soubirous girl who's claiming to have visions and upsetting everyone?"

Bernadette did not answer. She just stood up straight. The judge insisted, "Listen to me, my girl, this has gone on long enough. All of Lourdes is talking about nothing but you!"

"Too many people want to go watch when you visit the Massabielle grotto. One day there's going to be an accident. You must not go there anymore!"

Bernadette calmly replied, "I promised the Lady I'd go there till Thursday."

At this, the judge got angry. "I don't think you understood me. I forbid you to go back there. Otherwise, I'll throw you in prison!"

Bernadette, tight-lipped, shook her head no. After all, the judge had no right to put her in jail. She had not done anything wrong!

The very next day, Bernadette went back to Massabielle. As usual, there was a big crowd waiting. The muddy puddle from which she had drunk had grown larger. Bernadette had discovered a spring that no one before had known about.

One woman who was expecting a baby had even walked for miles to be there. Her name was Catherine Latapie. A few years before, she had fallen off a ladder she had climbed to gather nuts from a tree. Since then, she could no longer move her hand. As soon as Bernadette stood up after praying, Catherine plunged her hand into the water. It was incredible—she was able to move her fingers again! She quickly went back home because she felt she was about to have her baby.

The next day, tongues were wagging—there had been a miracle at the grotto! People did not think Bernadette was a liar anymore. But Bernadette's problems were not over, because now the Beautiful Lady had asked her to have a chapel built for her!

"I am the Immaculate Conception"

The very next day, Bernadette went to call on Father Peyramale. He was a rather grumpy old man, but Bernadette felt confident. If the Lady wanted a chapel, he could not refuse!

"Reverend Father, the Lady wants a chapel built for her and for everyone to go there in a procession."

"A chapel! A procession! And then what!" thundered the old man. "And why should I do anything for this lady whom I don't even know? Ask her first to tell us her name and to make the wild rosebush bloom in front of the grotto—and then we'll see!"

Father Peyramale was stubborn. He wanted proof that Bernadette was not just making up stories. So Bernadette did as he said. Three days in a row, she asked the Beautiful Lady to tell her her name and to make the wild rosebush bloom. But the Beautiful Lady merely gave Bernadette her most radiant smile.

Bernadette stopped going to the grotto for twenty days. She did not feel the Beautiful Lady was calling her. But one morning, she understood that she had to go back. As soon as the Lady appeared, Bernadette asked her the same question: "Could you tell me your name, please?" And this time, the Lady answered! She spread out her hands toward the ground as though in prayer and said in the local dialect, "I am the Immaculate Conception!"

Bernadette ran to Father Peyramale's house, repeating these words all along the way so she would not forget them. Because even though the Lady had spoken in her native language, Bernadette did not understand what she meant. As soon as the priest opened the door, she shouted the words, "I am the Immaculate Conception!"

Angrily, the priest said, "What is that, 'The Immaculate Conception'? Do you even know what that means?"

"No, but that's what the Lady told me!"

Father Peyramale was speechless. How could Bernadette, who did not even know how to read, who had hardly ever been to catechism, how could she know this name that the Church had only just given to the Virgin Mary a few years before? The priest was astounded … and he began to believe that this Lady was the Blessed Virgin. But he did not say anything yet to Bernadette, who insisted before she left, "And she still wants her chapel!"

$\mathcal{H}$undreds of people waited for Bernadette every day in front of the grotto. Everyone was talking about it!

"I ran into the Reverend Father and—he didn't want to say so—but he doesn't seem to think that Bernadette's talking nonsense anymore!" one lady whispered to her neighbor.

"I told you so! It's the Blessed Virgin that little one sees! It's miraculous!"

Next to these two gossips stood Doctor Dozous, who smiled and said, "It's the fruit of her imagination! She even thinks it's true herself!"

*B*efore beginning her prayer, Bernadette lit a candle. She cupped the little flame in her hand. Suddenly, her face lit up.

"This is it! She sees her!" whispered one lady.

"Oh, look! The poor thing's going to burn her hand on that candle!" cried another.

She got up to go help Bernadette, but Doctor Dozous stopped her. "Leave her alone, madam. If the girl is really seeing the Virgin, she can't come to any harm, can she?" he said.

The flame of the candle licked at Bernadette's hand for a long time, but she did not move! When she stood up again, Doctor Dozous hurried to her and asked, "Are you hurt? Show me your hand!"

Bernadette was surprised, but she did as he asked. Why was this man looking at her palm so carefully? There was nothing at all wrong with her hand!

The crowds at Massabielle had become so big that the police decided to fence off the grotto. Poor Bernadette! She would see the Blessed Virgin again only one last time, and from far away on the other side of the Gave River. But soon the bishop was to announce that Bernadette had been telling the truth. And he was going to have a chapel built, like the Virgin wanted.

As for Bernadette, she wanted to become a nun and entered a convent in Nevers, France, where she took the name Sister Marie-Bernard. Of course, all the sisters wanted to ask her loads of questions! But the mother superior did not in the least agree!

"Sister Marie-Bernard told us all about the apparitions the evening she arrived. I don't want to hear any more about it!"

Bernadette was relieved. She did not want people to think she was something special. One day, she said to one of the sisters who was amazed at her silence, "What do you do with a broom when you've finished sweeping? You put it back where it belongs, behind the door. And it's the same thing with me. The Blessed Virgin made use of me, and now I'm going back to the place where I belong."

And that place was the convent infirmary, where Bernadette took care of the sick: she comforted and consoled them, without ever complaining of being tired.

And yet, Bernadette was very ill. Ever since she was little, she had had a serious disease called tuberculosis. Soon she was not able to take care of the patients anymore. Instead, it was she who had to stay lying in bed in the infirmary. And there it was that she died and went to join God and the Blessed Virgin Mary, who had promised to make her happy in heaven.

On December 8, 1933, the Church declared her a saint. As with many of the saints, her body has remained untouched by death—Bernadette looks as if she is sleeping. Her body was placed in a big glass casket in Nevers, where many Christians go to pray.

But it is in the town of Lourdes that Bernadette is especially honored. You can visit "the dungeon", the little room where she lived with her whole family at the time of the apparitions. Thousands of pilgrims go there each year to pray at the grotto. Among them are those who follow in Bernadette's footsteps, helping, comforting, and tending to the sick.

In Lourdes, you can almost hear the words of Jesus, "Whatever you do for one of the least of these brothers of mine, you do for me."

JE NE VOUS PROMETS PAS LE BONHEUR EN CE MONDE MAIS DANS L'AUTRE

Feast Days

Saint Bernadette's feast day is February 18.
Our Lady of Lourdes is commemorated on February 11 because it was on that day in 1858
that the Blessed Virgin Mary appeared to Bernadette for the first time.

The Apparitions

The Blessed Virgin Mary appeared to Bernadette eighteen times between February 11 and July 16, 1858.

The Grotto of Lourdes

The little grotto of Lourdes has hardly changed at all since the apparitions.
Today, a statue can be seen in the cleft in the rocks where the Blessed Virgin appeared.
Pilgrims gather there to pray.

The Waters of Lourdes

Water still flows in the grotto. Pilgrims fill little bottles with it
or bathe in pools filled with this water. To bathe in or drink the water from the grotto
is an act of faith that God can transform hearts and even heal the sick.

The Miracles

The Church has recognized sixty-seven miraculous healings
through the intercession of Our Lady of Lourdes. The Church studies each case carefully
with doctors, so there can be no mistake.

The Immaculate Conception

This is the title given to Mary, who was born free from original sin.
Pope Pius IX had proclaimed the dogma of the Immaculate Conception in 1854,
but Bernadette did not know that. She did not even understand what the words meant.
That is how people knew that Bernadette was telling the truth.